A Crabtree Branches Book

Today's Stars

LEBRON JAMES

USA

Ellen Rodger

Crabtree Publishing
crabtreebooks.com

School-to-Home Support for Caregivers and Teachers

This high-interest book is designed to motivate striving students with engaging topics while building fluency, vocabulary, and an interest in reading. Here are a few questions and activities to help the reader build upon his or her comprehension skills.

Before Reading:

- *What do I think this book is about?*
- *What do I know about this topic?*
- *What do I want to learn about this topic?*
- *Why am I reading this book?*

During Reading:

- *I wonder why...*
- *I'm curious to know...*
- *How is this like something I already know?*
- *What have I learned so far?*

After Reading:

- *What was the author trying to teach me?*
- *What are some details?*
- *How did the photographs and captions help me understand more?*
- *Read the book again and look for the vocabulary words.*
- *What questions do I still have?*

Extension Activities:

- *What was your favorite part of the book? Write a paragraph on it.*
- *Draw a picture of your favorite thing you learned from the book.*

TABLE OF CONTENTS

TOP OF THE KEY

LeBron James is one of the greatest professional basketball players of all time. He's been given the nickname "King James" because his fans consider him a king of the court.

LeBron is a record-breaker both on and off the court.

In more than 20 years playing in the National Basketball Association (NBA), LeBron has won dozens of awards. He has also become one of the **wealthiest** players in the NBA.

LeBron is the NBA's leading scorer. He hit that mark in 2023, breaking a record set by NBA star Kareem Abdul-Jabbar in 1984.

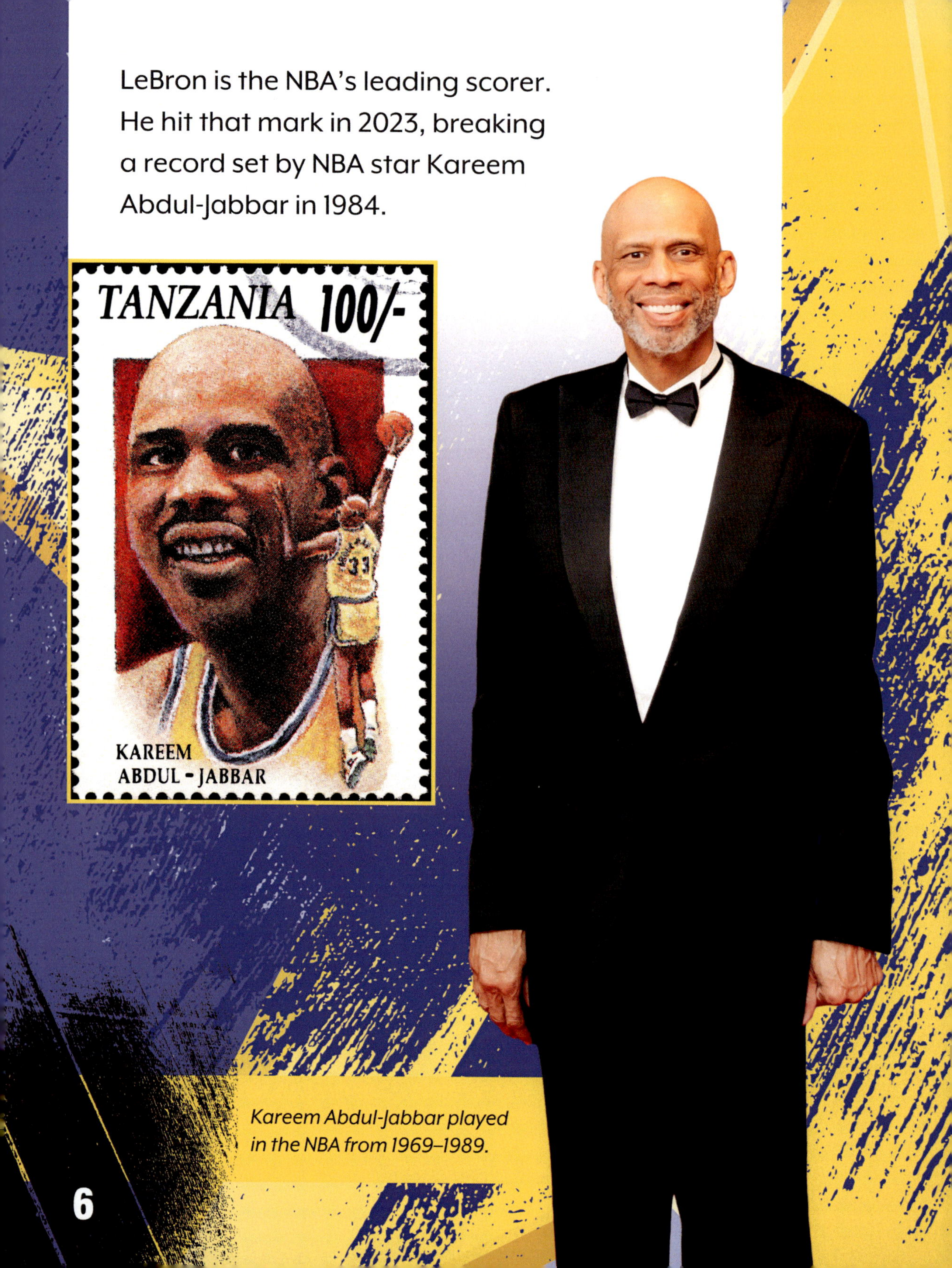

Kareem Abdul-Jabbar played in the NBA from 1969–1989.

Fun Facts

In his 22nd season with the NBA, LeBron signed a $100 million contract with the Los Angeles Lakers.

EARLY DAYS

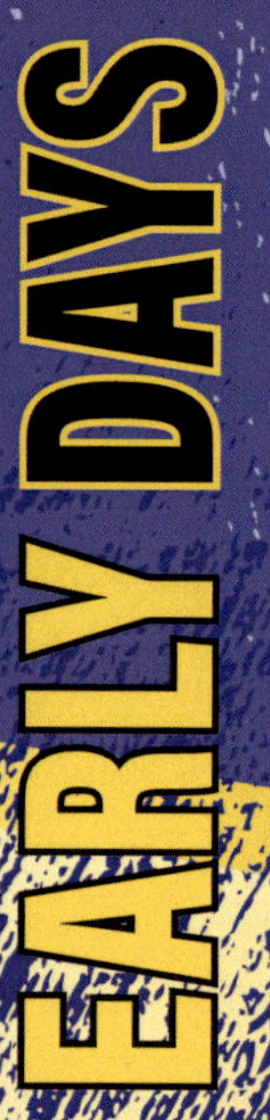

LeBron Raymone James was born on December 30, 1984, in Akron, Ohio. His mother, Gloria, was just 16 when he was born. Gloria raised him with the help of family and, later, LeBron's football coach.

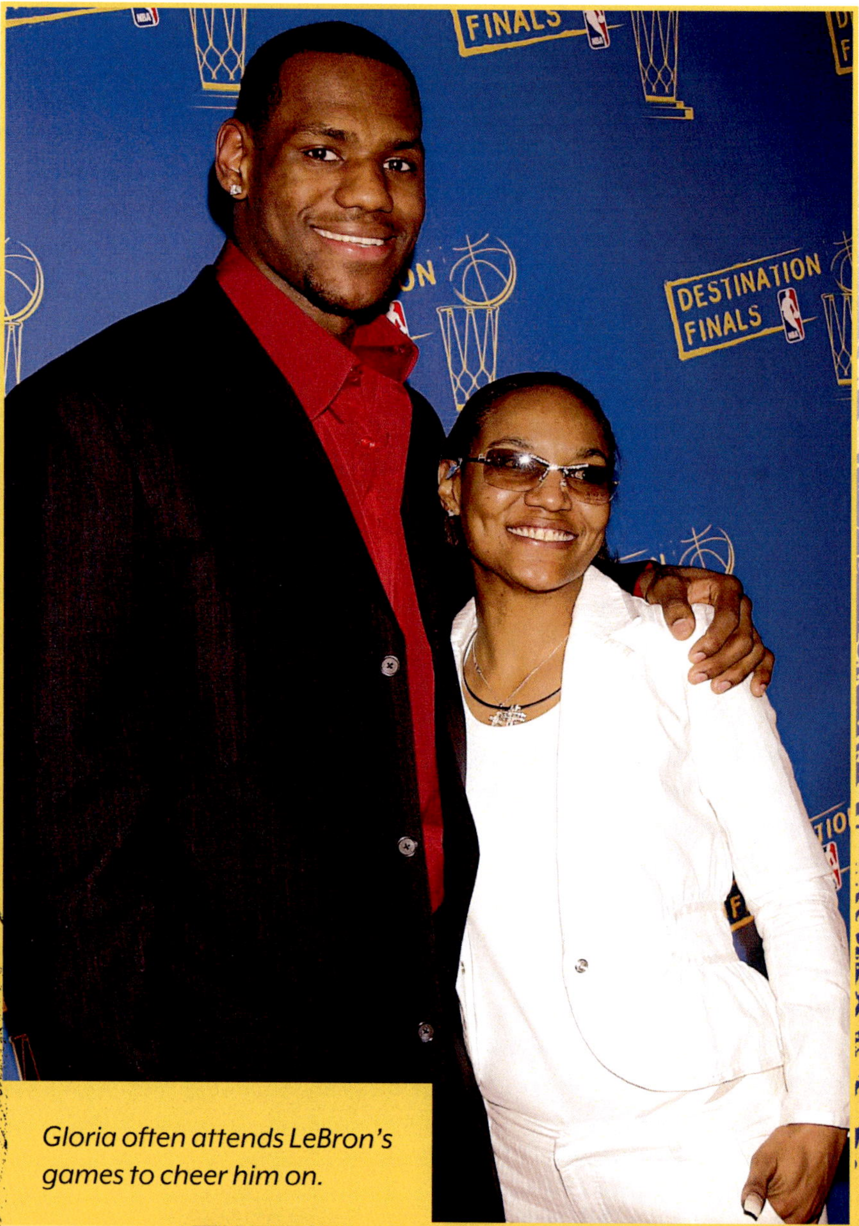

Gloria often attends LeBron's games to cheer him on.

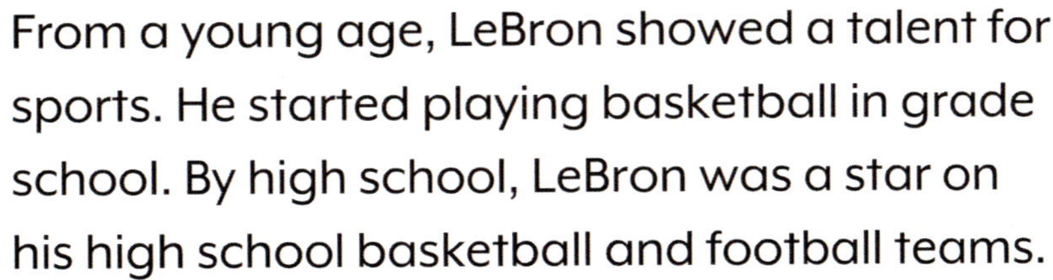

From a young age, LeBron showed a talent for sports. He started playing basketball in grade school. By high school, LeBron was a star on his high school basketball and football teams.

In high school, LeBron and four of his teammates were known as the Akron Fab Five. They made it to state and national championships.

LeBron and his high school team played highly **ranked** teams throughout the country. In his junior year, he was named Gatorade National Player of the Year.

After his junior year LeBron wanted to go straight to the NBA, but he needed to graduate high school first.

Fun Facts

LeBron was first featured on the cover of *Sports Illustrated* in his junior year of high school. He has since appeared on the cover more than 40 times.

RISING STAR

After he graduated high school, LeBron went straight to the NBA! He was the number one pick in the 2003 NBA **draft**. His team? The nearby Cleveland Cavaliers!

LeBron played for the Cavaliers for 11 seasons.

In his first NBA game, LeBron scored 25 points. He averaged 20 points per game throughout his **rookie** season. Everyone wanted to see LeBron play. He was named Rookie of the Year!

By his second season, LeBron was named to the NBA All-Star Team. He was just 20 years old. He also sorted through **endorsement** offers. Companies wanted LeBron associated with their products.

In 2005, Bubblicious bubble gum introduced a flavor called LeBron's Lightning Lemonade.

Fun Facts

LeBron married his high school sweetheart, Savannah. They have three children, LeBron Jr. (Bronny), Bryce, and Zhuri.

KING JAMES

Throughout his NBA career, LeBron has played for three teams. He started with the Cleveland Cavaliers (2003–2010 and 2014–2018). He played four seasons with the Miami Heat (2010–2014) and later signed with the Los Angeles Lakers (2018–).

LeBron's list of awards is long and impressive, and includes being named an NBA Most Valuable Player (MVP) four times. He holds the record for most NBA All Star selections, with 20 appearances!

LeBron has helped his teams win NBA championships four times.

As the oldest active player in the NBA, LeBron keeps himself fit to continue playing well. His training **regimen** includes weightlifting, yoga, and running.

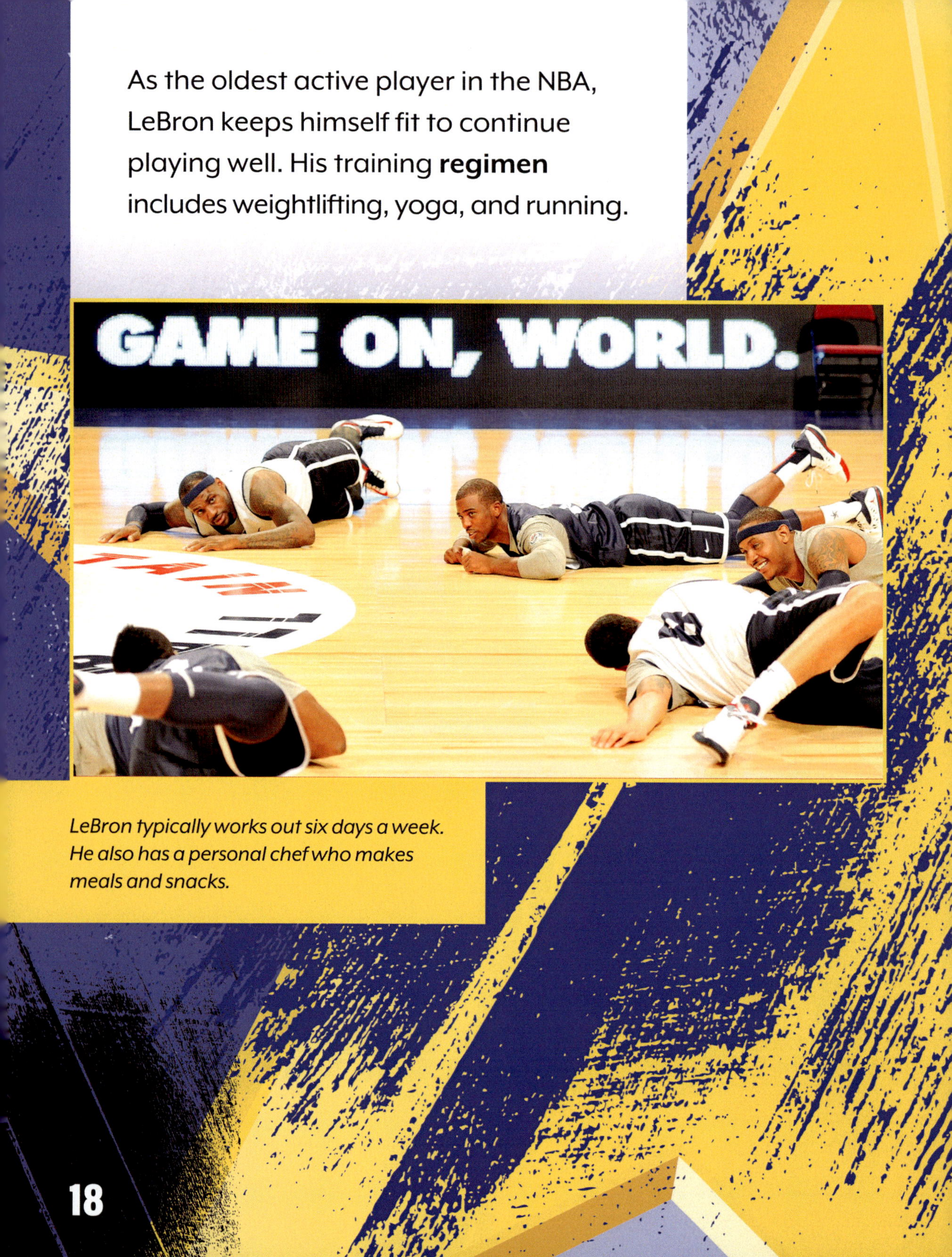

LeBron typically works out six days a week. He also has a personal chef who makes meals and snacks.

Fun Facts

On game days, LeBron likes to eat a peanut butter and jelly sandwich before playing. The peanut butter gives him energy.

OLYMPIC ATHLETE

LeBron represented the United States as a member of the U.S. national team in four Olympic Games. He won a bronze medal with Team USA at the 2004 Games in Athens, Greece.

At 19, LeBron was the youngest member of the 2004 U.S. Olympic basketball team.

At the 2008 Olympic Games in Beijing, China, LeBron and Team USA won gold. Four years later, in 2012, LeBron was a member of the gold-medal-winning Olympic team in London, UK. In 2024, LeBron won gold again in Paris, France.

LeBron was 39 at the 2024 Olympics, making him the oldest U.S. Olympic basketball player.

LeBron's love for the game has carried him through decades in the NBA. It also guides his style of play. On court, he has a vision and he sees it through.

LeBron has played more seasons than many other basketball greats.

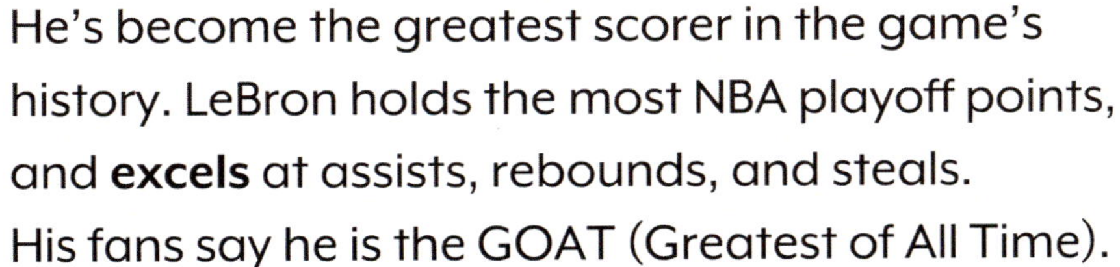

He's become the greatest scorer in the game's history. LeBron holds the most NBA playoff points, and **excels** at assists, rebounds, and steals. His fans say he is the GOAT (Greatest of All Time).

DYNASTY MAKER

One of LeBron's "firsts" was playing in the NBA with his son Bronny, who was drafted by the Los Angeles Lakers in 2024. LeBron and Bronny are the NBA's first father-son duo to play on the same team at the same time.

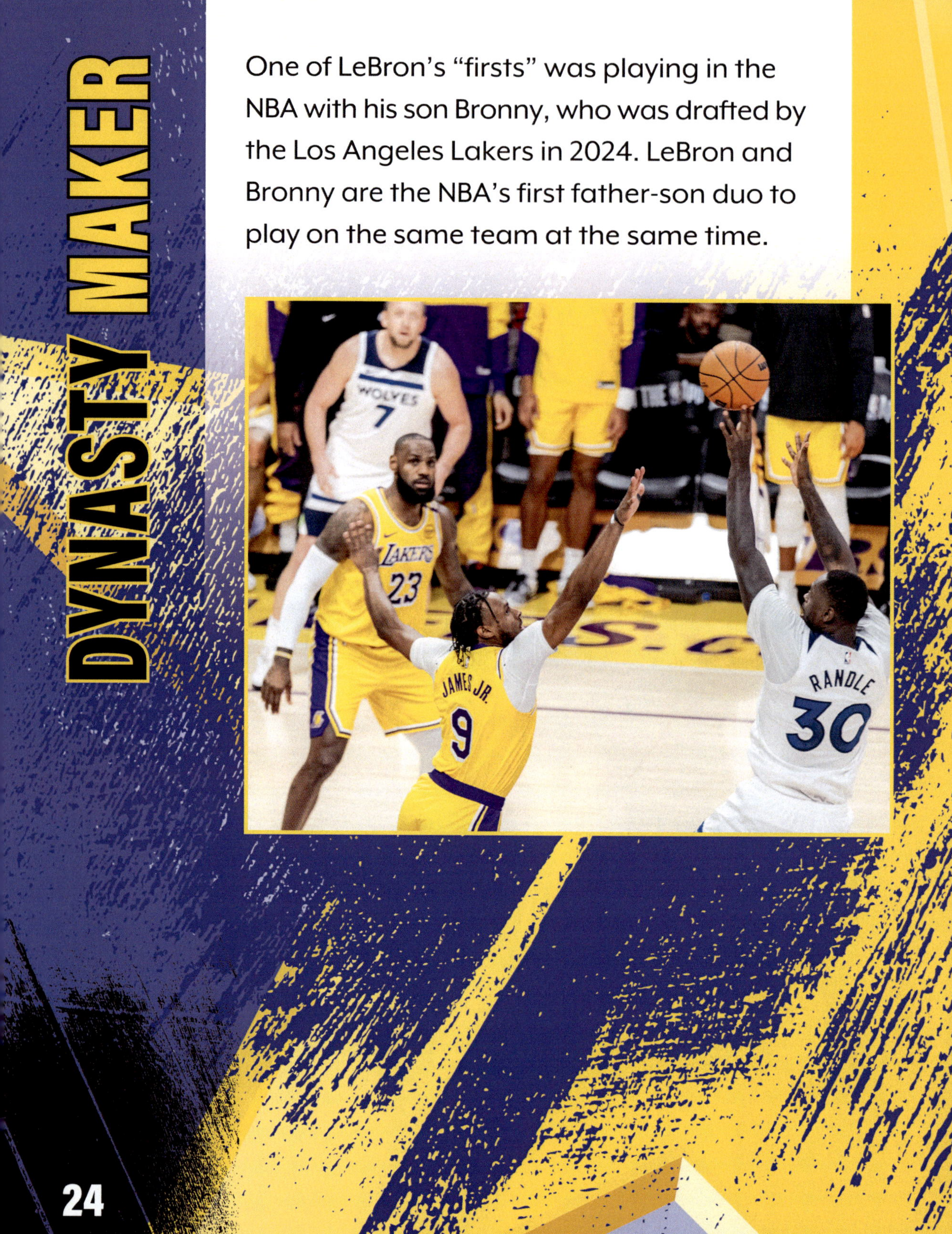

Early in his career, LeBron began endorsing products for companies such as Nike and Coca-Cola. As his **fame** and earnings grew, he became the highest-paid basketball player in the world.

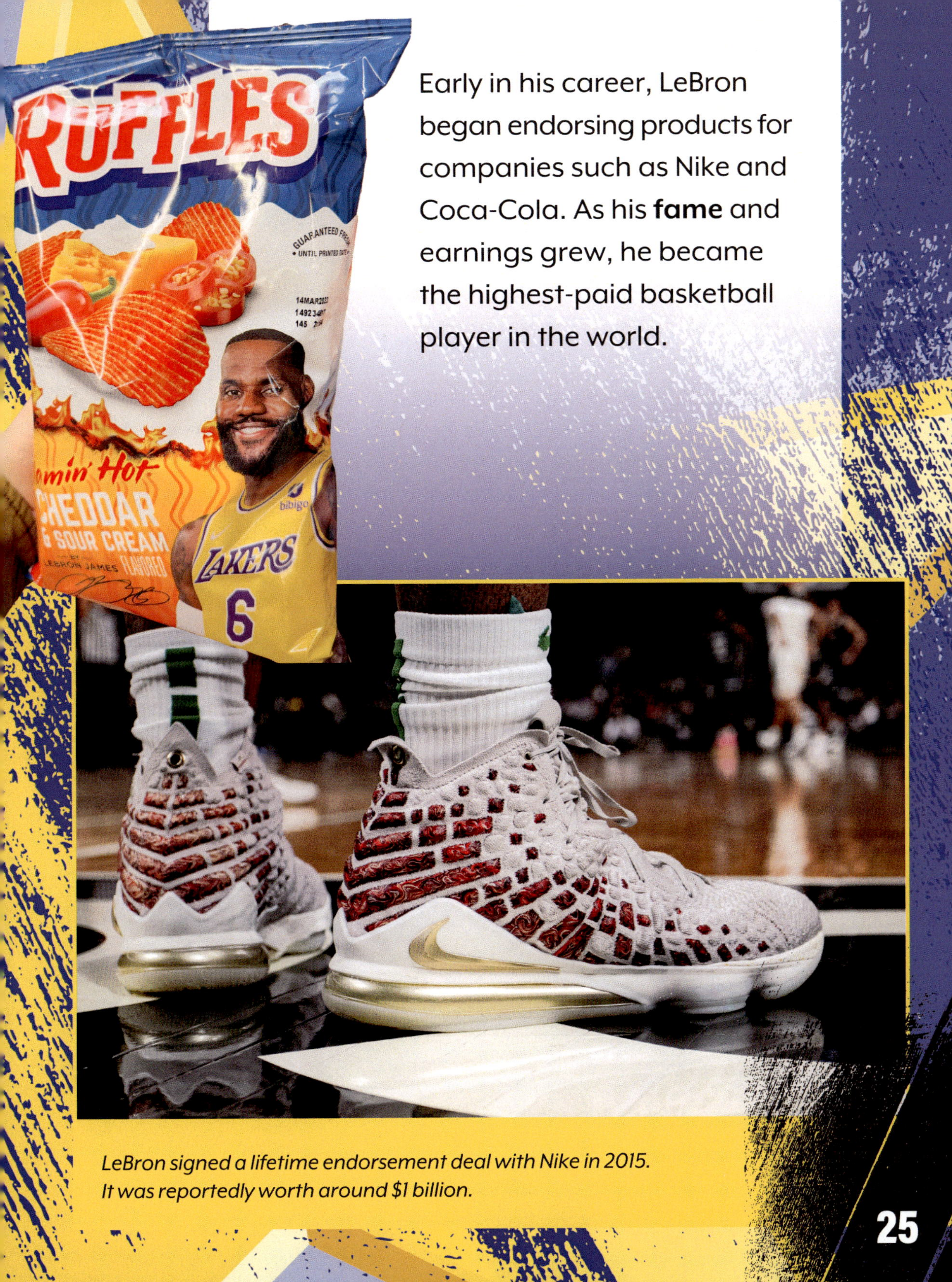

LeBron signed a lifetime endorsement deal with Nike in 2015. It was reportedly worth around $1 billion.

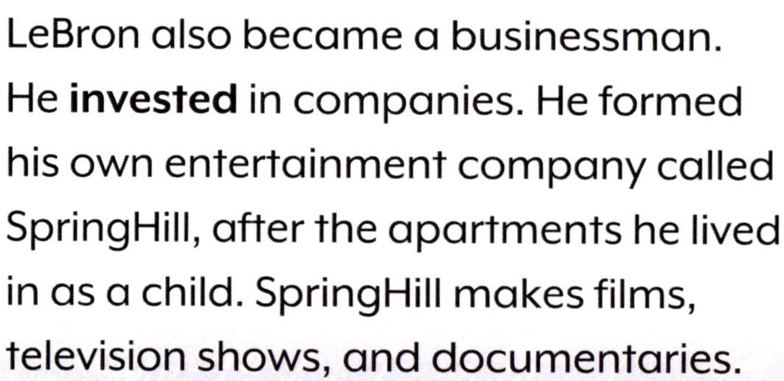

LeBron also became a businessman. He **invested** in companies. He formed his own entertainment company called SpringHill, after the apartments he lived in as a child. SpringHill makes films, television shows, and documentaries.

*In 2015, LeBron was elected as the first vice president of the National Basketball Players Association (NBPA). This is a **union** that supports NBA players.*

Fun Facts

LeBron is a part owner of the Boston Red Sox and the Liverpool Football Club.

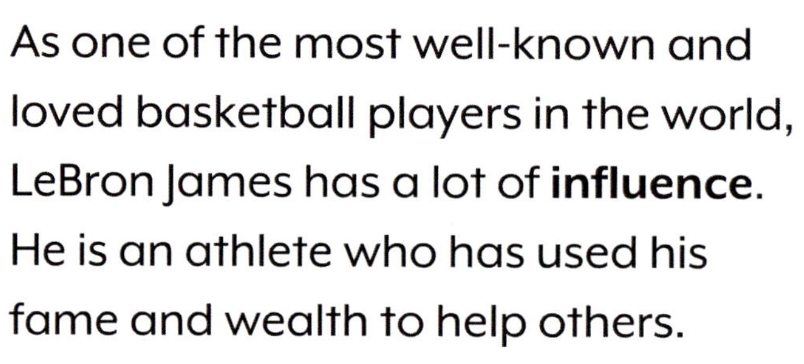

As one of the most well-known and loved basketball players in the world, LeBron James has a lot of **influence**. He is an athlete who has used his fame and wealth to help others.

LeBron appears in around 2 million Google searches each month. He has a massive social media following.

LeBron didn't have a lot as a kid. Basketball and business made him successful as an adult. Today he shares his wealth and **promotes** many causes to "give back" to his community and the world.

In 2004, LeBron set up the LeBron James Family Foundation to help build stronger communities and families in Akron, Ohio.

GLOSSARY

draft (draft): A process in which sports teams take turns selecting from a group of players

endorsement (en-DAWRS-muhnt): The act of publicly saying that you like a product in exchange for money

excel (ek-SEL): To be or do better than others

fame (feym): The quality of being well known by many people

influence (IN-floo-uhns): The power to have an important effect on someone or something

invested (in-VEST-ed): Put money to use in something offering income or profit

promote (pruh-MOHT): To help or encourage something to do well

ranked (rangkt): An official position or standing

regimen (REJ-uh-men): A system or regulated course of diet, exercise, and way of living that is meant to preserve health and strength

rookie (ROOK-ee): An athlete playing their first season in a professional sport

union (YOON-yuhn): An organization of workers who have joined together to protect their working rights

wealthiest (WEL-thee-ist): Among the most rich

INDEX

WEBSITES TO VISIT

https://www.nba.com/player/2544/lebron-james

https://www.biography.com/athletes/lebron-james

https://www.lebronjamesfamilyfoundation.org

ABOUT THE AUTHOR

Ellen Rodger won a bank-sponsored short story contest at age nine. It was the last thing her bank ever gave her for free, but it kicked-started a career in newspaper, magazine, and book publishing. Ellen has written hundreds of books for curious young people, on topics as varied as the history of the potato, urban wildlife, refugees, the Great Lakes, and explorers.

Crabtree Publishing

crabtreebooks.com 800-387-7650

Written by: Ellen Rodger
Designed by: Kathy Walsh
Series Development: James Earley
Editor: Melissa Boyce
Educational Consultant: Marie Lemke M.Ed.
Production manager: Candice Campbell

Hardcover: 978-1-0398-8032-0
Paperback: 978-1-0398-8392-5
Ebook (pdf): 978-1-0398-8152-5
Epub: 978-1-0398-8272-0

Printed in the U.S.A./CP2025

Published in Canada
Crabtree Publishing
616 Welland Ave.
St. Catharines, Ontario
L2M 5V6

Published in the United States
Crabtree Publishing
347 Fifth Ave
Suite 1402-145
New York, NY 10016

Library and Archives Canada Cataloguing in Publication
Available at Library and Archives Canada

Library of Congress Cataloging-in-Publication Data
Available at the Library of Congress

Photographs
Alamy: UPI p 7, 21, ZUMA p 8, 14, Cinematic Collection p 9, Martin Rickett p 18, SOPA Images p 24, PjrStudio p 28, A.J. Sisco p 29
Newscom: Bob Falcetti p 10, GDA Photo Service p 11, NELSON CHING p 12, David Santiago p 16, 17, Sandra Teddy p 20
Shutterstock: A.RICARDO, cover, title page, p 5, p 19, p 22, p 23; Lester Balajadia, TOC; Tinseltown, p 4; patuletail, p 6 (left); Rena Schild, p 6 (right); Scott Meivogel, p 13; Kathy Hutchins, p 15; ZikG, p 25 (top); 1022 Project, p 25 (bottom); Cristian Storto, p 26; mourizativa, p 27 (top); Marcio Jose Bastos Silva, p 27 (bottom)
All other images from Shutterstock